Learn E

Practical Guide

A. De Quattro

Practical Guide Erlang

Introduction

Erlang is a programming language and runtime system designed for building distributed, concurrent, and highly available applications. Originally developed in the 1980s at the Ericsson Computer Science Laboratory, it was created to address the needs of telephony and telecommunications. With a focus on fault tolerance, scalability, and ease of modification, Erlang has emerged as a go-to language for developing complex and critical applications.

Chapter 1: What is Erlang?

Erlang is a functional programming language, but it also includes features that make it suitable for concurrent and distributed programming. It is designed to develop applications requiring continuous availability and the ability to handle tens of thousands of lightweight processes simultaneously. Erlang's syntax is influenced by languages such as Prolog and Ada, but its structure is unique.

One of Erlang's distinguishing features is its concurrency model based on the "actor model," where processes communicate with each other via messages rather than shared state. This approach enables the construction of highly responsive and resilient applications through process separation and state management.

Erlang is also known for its Garbage Collection, which efficiently manages memory and allows programmers to focus on application logic without worrying excessively about memory management.

1.1 History of Erlang

Erlang was designed in the early 1980s at Ericsson by Joe Armstrong, Robert Virding, and Mike Williams. The need for a language capable of managing the complex operations of telecommunications led to the creation of Erlang. In 1986, the language was first implemented as part of a research project, and in 1998, it was released as open-source software.

This marked a significant turning point in the language's history, as the community could contribute to its development and improvement. Over the years, Erlang has seen increasing adoption in telecommunications and the software development industry, where it has been used to build critical applications like WhatsApp, which handles billions of messages daily.

1.2 Why Use Erlang?

There are several reasons to consider Erlang for developing a new application:

1. **Reliability**: Erlang is designed to handle errors effectively. Its fault tolerance allows building systems that do not crash due

to errors in a single component, ensuring continuous operation even in the face of failures.

2. **Scalability**: With support for concurrency at the level of lightweight processes, Erlang can manage hundreds of thousands of simultaneous processes, making it ideal for scalable applications like messaging servers or real-time web applications.

3. **Rapid Development**: Thanks to its functional nature and automated memory management, developers can focus more on business logic than implementation details, speeding up the development cycle.

4. **Robust Ecosystem**: Erlang has a growing ecosystem with numerous libraries and tools that simplify application development. The most notable framework is "OTP" (Open Telecom Platform), which provides libraries and tools for building robust applications.

5. **Support for Distributed Systems**: Erlang was born as a language for programming distributed systems. Its

architecture makes it easy to manage the distribution of processes across multiple nodes, facilitating the creation of scalable applications.

1.3 Key Features

Erlang offers a range of key features that make it a strong choice for production software:

- **Lightweight Process Model**: Erlang processes are lightweight compared to traditional threads, allowing for the easy creation of a large number of simultaneous processes.

- **Messaging**: Processes communicate by sending and receiving messages, avoiding state conflicts and simplifying the construction of concurrent systems.

- **Error Handling**: Erlang's "let it crash" model encourages developers to write straightforward code and handle errors by restarting processes, simplifying application control flow.

- **Garbage Collection**: Automated memory management via garbage collection makes the language user-friendly and reduces the likelihood of memory leaks common in other languages.

- **Hot Code Swapping**: This feature enables developers to update running code without interrupting the application, making maintenance and the release of new features simpler.

- **Cloud Compatibility**: Applications written in Erlang integrate well with cloud architectures, making the language adaptable to modern development paradigms.

1.4 Installation and Configuration

Installing Erlang is a straightforward process, varying slightly depending on the operating system used.

1.5 On Unix/Linux

1. **Using a Package Manager**: Most Linux distributions have precompiled Erlang packages in their repositories. For Ubuntu, you can use the command:

```bash
sudo apt-get install erlang
```

2. **Compiling from Source**: If you want the latest version or a customized configuration, you can download the source code from Erlang's official site and compile it. Here's an example:

```bash
wget https://github.com/erlang/otp/releases/download/<version>/otp_<version>.tar.gz

tar -xzvf otp_<version>.tar.gz

cd otp_<version>

./configure

make

sudo make install
```

1.5.1 On Windows

To install Erlang on Windows, follow these steps:

1. **Download the Installer**: Visit Erlang's website and download the Windows installer.

2. **Run the Installer**: Follow the installer's instructions. Ensure you add Erlang to your

system's PATH to run it from any terminal.

3. **Verify the Installation**: After installation, verify that Erlang is installed correctly by opening a terminal and typing:

```bash
erl
```

You should see the Erlang interactive shell if the installation was successful.

1.5.2 Configuring the Development Environment

Once Erlang is installed, you can use the interactive shell to test code. However, for larger projects, it is common to use tools like Rebar or Mix (used in Elixir, which runs on Erlang) to manage dependencies and the build process.

To start a new project with Rebar:

```bash
rebar3 new app my_app
cd my_app
```

This command generates a basic project structure with the necessary files to begin developing your application. You can then modify the files and start the server with:

```bash
rebar3 shell
```

Erlang offers a unique combination of features that make it particularly suitable for developing distributed and highly available systems. Its long history in the telecommunications industry and a robust developer community make it an attractive choice for critical applications. Whether you are developing a web application, a messaging system, or any application requiring scalability and reliability, Erlang is a strong option. With its intuitive interface and powerful features, it is a language worth exploring.

Chapter 2: Fundamentals of Erlang

Erlang is a functional programming language designed primarily for building distributed, highly available systems. Its syntax is simple, and its philosophy revolves around concurrency, long-term application development, and fault tolerance. In this section, we will explore the fundamentals of Erlang, divided into various subsections covering basic syntax, data types, operators, functions, and control structures.

2.0 Basic Syntax

The syntax of Erlang is unique and distinct from many other programming languages. An Erlang program consists of one or more modules. Each module is defined using the `-module` keyword and the module's name, followed by the `-export` keyword to specify which functions are accessible externally.

Example of a Simple Module

```erlang
-module(example).
```

```erlang
-export([greet/1]).

greet(Name) ->
io:format("Hello, ~s!~n", [Name]).
```

In this example, we define a module named `example` and a function `greet` that accepts a string argument `Name`. The function uses `io:format` to print a greeting message.

2.1 Data Types

Erlang has several fundamental data types that can be used in programming. Below, we describe some of the main data types.

2.2 Numbers

Erlang supports integers and floating-point numbers. Integers can be both positive and negative. Examples of numbers include:

```erlang
1. % positive integer

-5. % negative integer

3.14. % floating-point number
```

2.2.1 Atoms

Atoms are constants representing unique names. They are similar to strings but are immutable and used for identifying states and types. Atoms always begin with a lowercase letter or are enclosed in single quotes.

```erlang
player.

'Outstanding_Player'.
```

2.2.2 Lists

Lists in Erlang are ordered collections of elements that can be of different types. The syntax for lists uses square brackets, and elements are separated by commas.

```erlang
NumberList = [1, 2, 3, 4, 5].

MixedList = [1, atom, "string", [4, 5]].
```

2.2.3 Tuples

Tuples are similar to lists but are used to group a fixed number of elements of any type. Tuples are defined using curly braces.

```erlang
Tuple = {1, atom, "text"}.
```

2.2.4 Maps

Maps are collections of key-value pairs. Keys can be of any type, and the map is defined using `%{}`. Maps provide faster access to values compared to lists.

```erlang
Map = #{name => "Mario", age => 30, city => "Rome"}.
```

2.3 Operators

Erlang provides a range of operators for various purposes, including:

- **Arithmetic Operators**: `+`, `-`, `*`, `/`, `div`, `rem`

- **Logical Operators**: `and`, `or`, `not`

- **Comparison Operators**: `==`, `/=`, `=:=`, `=/=`, `<`, `>`, `=<`, `>=`

- **Sequence Operators**: `;`, `,`

Example of Operator Usage

```erlang
Sum = 5 + 3.

Average = Sum div 2.

Comparison = 5 > 3.
```

2.4 Functions

Erlang is a functional language, making functions one of its key design elements.

2.4.1 Defining a Function

Functions in Erlang are defined using the `->` operator, with the function name, arguments, and body. An example function definition is as follows:

```erlang
team(Points) ->

case Points of

X when X >= 90 -> "Excellent";

X when X >= 75 -> "Good";

_ -> "Improve!"

end.
```

2.4.2 Anonymous Functions

Erlang allows the use of anonymous functions, which can be created easily. These are defined using the `fun` keyword:

```erlang
Sum = fun(X, Y) -> X + Y end.

Result = Sum(3, 5).
```

2.5 Control Structures

Erlang uses control structures to manage the program's flow.

2.5.1 Conditions

Conditions in Erlang can be managed through `if`, `case`, or `cond`. Here is an example of using `case`:

```erlang
draw(Color) ->

case Color of

red -> "Draw a red circle.";

blue -> "Draw a blue square.";

_ -> "Unrecognized color."
```

end.
```

#### 2.5.2 Loops

Erlang does not have traditional loop constructs like `for` or `while`, but recursion can be used to implement loops. Below is an example of recursion that calculates the factorial of a number:

```erlang
factorial(0) -> 1;

factorial(N) when N > 0 -> N * factorial(N - 1).
```

Erlang is a powerful and versatile language for concurrent and distributed programming, with simple syntax and robust data type management. Its core types, such as numbers, atoms, lists, tuples, and maps, provide a solid foundation for building complex applications.

Its functions, both defined and anonymous, allow developers to write clear and modular code, while control structures like conditions and recursion offer the flexibility needed to
```

manage program logic. Despite an initial learning curve, Erlang is highly valued in applications requiring high availability and fault tolerance, standing out in the modern programming landscape with a reputation for reliability and stability.

Chapter 3: Conceptual Programming

Erlang is a programming language designed for building distributed and highly available systems. Programming in Erlang relies on fundamental concepts that are distinctive and unique compared to other languages. In this section, we will explore the core principles of conceptual programming in Erlang, covering modules and functions, pattern matching, recursion, and error handling.

3.1 Modules and Functions

Modules

In Erlang, modules are fundamental units for organizing code. A module is simply a file containing function definitions and optionally other elements like records and types. Modules are used to group related functions and provide a clear and organized interface.

Modules in Erlang must have a name corresponding to the file name. For example, a module named `math_operations` must be saved in a file called `math_operations.erl`. Within a module, you can define functions using the following syntax:

```erlang
-module(math_operations). % Module definition

-export([add/2, subtract/2]). % Exporting functions

add(X, Y) -> % Function to add two numbers
X + Y.

subtract(X, Y) -> % Function to subtract two numbers
X - Y.
```

Functions

Functions in Erlang are unique because they not only perform computations but also support functional programming. You can define private functions, usable only within the module, and public functions, which can be invoked by other modules.

Functions can include pattern matching, allowing for highly modular function definitions. Consider the following example, which calculates the factorial of a number using recursion:

```erlang
-module(factorial).

-export([fact/1]).

fact(0) -> 1; % Base case

fact(N) when N > 0 -> N * fact(N - 1). % Recursive case
```

In this example, `fact/1` combines the base case `fact(0)` and the recursive case `fact(N - 1)` to calculate the factorial of `N`.

3.2 Pattern Matching

Pattern matching is a distinctive feature of Erlang that simplifies code and improves readability. In traditional imperative programming, you might use `if` conditions to control program flow. In Erlang, you can use pattern matching to elegantly decompose and compare structures.

Here's a practical example:

```erlang
-module(item).
```

```erlang
-export([describe_item/1]).

describe_item({book, Title, Author}) ->
io:format("Book: ~s by ~s~n", [Title,
Author]);

describe_item({cd, Title, Artist}) ->
io:format("CD: ~s by ~s~n", [Title, Artist]);

describe_item(_) ->
io:format("Unknown item type~n").
```

In the code above, `describe_item/1` uses
pattern matching to distinguish between a
book, a CD, and other forms of input. If it
receives a tuple with the type and details, it
executes the appropriate block.

Another powerful example of pattern
matching is its use in lists:

```erlang
search_in_list([], _) -> false; % Base case:
empty list

search_in_list([H | T], X) when H =:= X ->
true; % Case: found

search_in_list([_ | T], X) -> search_in_list(T,
```

X). % Case: continue search

```
```

In the code above, `search_in_list/2` searches for an element in a list. It uses pattern matching to separate the head (H) and tail (T), allowing for recursive exploration of the list.

3.3 Recursion

Recursion is a fundamental concept in functional programming and is widely used in Erlang. It allows functions to call themselves directly or indirectly to solve problems. Recursion is often more elegant and clear compared to traditional iterative approaches.

Here's a complex example of recursion that calculates the sum of elements in a list:

```erlang
-module(list_sum).

-export([sum/1]).

sum([]) -> 0; % Base case: sum of an empty list is 0

sum([H | T]) -> H + sum(T). % Recursive case
```

In this example, `sum/1` uses pattern matching to handle the base case when the list is empty. If there are elements, the function adds the head (H) to the sum of the tail (T).

Recursion in Erlang is essential for working with complex data structures and must be used carefully to avoid stack overflow, which can occur with deep recursion. To address this issue, you can use techniques like tail recursion, where the last operation of the function is a call to itself. This allows the compiler to optimize memory usage.

Here's an example of tail recursion to calculate the sum:

```erlang
-module(tail_recursive_sum).

-export([sum/1]).

sum(List) -> sum_helper(List, 0).

sum_helper([], Acc) -> Acc; % Base case

sum_helper([H | T], Acc) -> sum_helper(T, Acc + H). % Recursive case
```

In this code, the helper function `sum_helper/2` uses an accumulator to store the partial result, avoiding the accumulation of calls on the stack.

3.4 Error Handling

Error handling in Erlang is a crucial part of programming, given the importance of reliability in distributed systems. Erlang adopts a "fail early" and "let it crash" approach, allowing processes to fail without compromising the entire system.

3.4.1 Try/Catch Constructs

Erlang provides a `try/catch` construct to handle exceptional situations. Through this construct, you can isolate sections of code that might generate errors and provide handling logic for various types of exceptions.

Here's an example showing how to use try/catch:

```erlang
-module(exception_example).

-export([divide/2]).

divide(X, 0) ->
```

```
{error, division_by_zero}; % Handle division
by zero

divide(X, Y) ->

try

X / Y

catch

error:badarg -> {error, bad_argument} %
Handle errors

end.
```

In this snippet, if you attempt to divide by
zero, `divide/2` will return an error, while if
the argument provided is valid, it performs the
division.

3.4.2 Idiomatic Error Handling

The idiomatic approach to handling errors in
Erlang involves evaluating the results of
operations rather than using exceptions. This
behavior is supported by using tuples of the
type `{ok, Result}` or `{error, Reason}`. This
pattern not only clarifies error handling but
also provides a robust way to propagate error
states through function calls.

A common example is the file system module, where functions return tuples:

```erlang
-module(file_operations).

-export([read_file/1]).

read_file(FileName) ->

case file:read_file(FileName) of

{ok, Content} -> {ok, Content};

{error, Reason} -> {error, Reason}

end.
```

In this case, `read_file/1` reads the content of a file and handles the result based on the operation's response. If successful, it returns the content; otherwise, it returns the error.

This approach makes the code easier to maintain and more lexically robust, enabling developers to handle every error scenario in a defined and visible way.

Erlang promotes robust and highly reliable development through the use of modules, pattern matching, and recursion. Error handling, whether through `try/catch` constructs or result evaluation, represents a best practice reflecting the core design principles for resilient systems tailored to the era of distributed computing. Through its uniqueness and diversity compared to other programming languages, Erlang provides the tools necessary to tackle challenges in developing scalable and durable applications.

Chapter 4 Concurrency in Erlang

4.1 Introduction to Concurrency

Erlang is a programming language designed for concurrent and distributed computation. Its architecture is based on a concurrency model that utilizes lightweight processes, unlike threads or operating system processes, which are heavier and more resource-intensive. Concurrency in Erlang is one of its defining features, enabling scalable and resilient applications capable of handling massive workloads and ensuring high availability.

Concurrent Processing Model

In Erlang, each process operates independently and communicates with others via messages. Each process has its own state and memory, meaning there are no memory conflicts unless processes interact directly. This model aligns well with modern application requirements, such as handling large numbers of simultaneous requests without blocking.

4.2 Erlang Processes

An Erlang process is a lightweight execution entity. Unlike traditional multiprocessing applications, where threads and processes are heavier and more complex, Erlang processes are designed to be extremely lightweight. A single Erlang system can manage tens of thousands or even millions of processes.

Process Creation

Processes in Erlang are created using the `spawn/1` or `spawn/3` function, which creates a new process from a function. The new process executes the function independently of its creator's environment. Here's an example:

```erlang
-module(my_module).

-export([start/0, worker/0]).

start() ->

Pid = spawn(fun worker/0), % Create a new process

Pid.

worker() ->

receive
```

```
{self(), Message} -> % Wait for a message
io:format("Received message: ~p~n",
[Message])
end.
```

In this example, the `my_module` module creates a new process (the "worker") that waits to receive a message. The `self()` function returns the PID of the calling process, which can be used to send messages to the child process.

4.3 Process Creation and Management

Process management in Erlang goes beyond creation and includes strategies such as supervision and lifecycle management.

Monitoring and Supervision

Erlang encourages a decentralized supervision strategy. Any process can monitor others and react to crashes or interruptions. Supervisors are special processes that control and manage groups of processes to ensure the system remains healthy.

Here is a simplified example of a supervisor:

```erlang
-module(supervisor).
-export([start/0, supervisor/0, worker/0]).
start() ->
spawn(fun supervisor/0).
supervisor() ->
WorkerPid = spawn(fun worker/0),
watch(WorkerPid).
watch(Pid) ->
receive
{'DOWN', Pid, _Reason} ->
io:format("Child process has stopped.~n")
end.
worker() ->
% Simulate worker behavior
timer:sleep(1000),
exit(normal).
```

In this example, the supervisor creates a worker and monitors its state. If the worker terminates, the supervisor sends a message to the monitoring handler.

4.4 Inter-Process Communication

In Erlang, processes communicate with each other using messages. This approach allows for great flexibility, enabling processes to remain independent.

4.4.1 Messages

Messages are simple data that can be sent between processes. A process can send a message to another process using the `!` (send) operator. Here's an example of sending a message:

```erlang
send_message(Pid, Message) ->

Pid ! Message.
```

In this case, the process `Pid` will receive `Message` if it is listening.

4.4.2 Message Queues

Every Erlang process has a "message queue" where messages are stored while waiting to be processed. When a process calls `receive`, messages are extracted from the queue in the order they arrived. This mechanism allows processes to handle messages in an orderly and non-blocking manner.

Here's an example of a process managing a message queue:

```erlang
handle_messages() ->

receive

{From, Msg} ->

io:format("Message from ~p: ~p~n", [From, Msg]),

handle_messages(); % Handle additional messages

after 5000 ->

io:format("No messages received in 5 seconds.~n")

end.
```

In this code, the process waits for messages from other processes and handles them one at a time.

4.5 Supervisors and Recovery Strategies

Resilience is a key characteristic of applications written in Erlang. Supervisors play a crucial role in ensuring processes are restarted in case of errors.

Recovery Strategies

Supervisors can follow different recovery strategies, which determine how applications respond to failures. Examples of strategies include:

1. **Restarting the process**: Restart the failed process.

2. **Terminating the process**: Stop the failing process without restarting it.

3. **Ignoring the failure**: If the failure is deemed non-critical, the supervisor can ignore it.

Here's an example of a supervisor with a recovery strategy:

```erlang
-module(simple_supervisor).

-export([start/0, supervise/1]).

start() ->
```

```erlang
spawn(fun() -> supervise(0) end).

supervise(Count) ->

case Count < 3 of % Attempt to restart 3 times

true ->

Pid = spawn(fun() -> worker(Count) end),

monitor(Pid),

supervise(Count + 1);

false ->

io:format("Max attempts reached, stopping
supervision.~n")

end.

monitor(Pid) ->

receive

{'DOWN', Pid, _Reason} ->

io:format("Worker has stopped.~n")

end.

worker(Count) ->

timer:sleep(1000),

exit(normal).

```

4.6 Actors and the Actor Model

The actor model is one of the most influential concurrency models, widely used in languages like Erlang. Each actor is an autonomous entity that can receive and send messages, as well as reuse states independently.

Features of the Actor Model

1. **Encapsulation of State**: Actors do not share their state with others, preventing concurrency conflicts.

2. **Message-based Communication**: Actors only communicate via message passing, ensuring a clear separation between computation and communication.

3. **Independence**: Actors operate independently, enabling high scalability.

Here's a practical example of the actor model in Erlang:

```erlang
-module(actor_example).

-export([start/0, actor/1]).

start() ->

Pid = spawn(fun() -> actor(0) end),
```

```erlang
Pid ! {self(), "Hello, Actor!"}.

actor(State) ->

receive

{Sender, Message} ->

io:format("Received from ~p: ~p ~n",
[Sender, Message]),

actor(State + 1);

after 2000 ->

io:format("Actor idle for 2 seconds,
terminating.~n")

end.
```

In this example, an actor can receive messages and process its state independently. By invoking `actor/1`, the process accepts messages from other actors and interacts with them without affecting its own state.

Conclusion

Erlang offers a powerful and flexible concurrency model suitable for building distributed systems requiring high availability and fault tolerance. The process-based organization allows efficient handling of complex workloads, using supervisors and recovery strategies to ensure integrity and stability. With support for the actor model, developers can focus on application design, leaving much of the concurrent process management to Erlang. This makes Erlang an excellent tool for creating robust, scalable, and resilient systems.

Chapter 5: Data Structures and Modules in Erlang

The Erlang programming language is designed for creating distributed and highly available systems. In this context, data structures and modules are fundamental elements that facilitate data management and code organization. In this section, we will explore the main data structures available in Erlang, their manipulation methods, and the creation and use of modules.

5.1 Lists and Manipulation Methods

Lists are one of the most commonly used data structures in Erlang. A list is a collection of elements that can be of any type. In Erlang, lists are represented as sequences of distinct elements, so they can contain other lists, tuples, or even maps.

Creating Lists

To create a list in Erlang, square brackets [] are used. Here are some examples of lists:

erlang

Copia

Modifica

ListOfNumbers = [1, 2, 3, 4, 5].

ListOfStrings = ["Erlang", "is", "awesome"].

MixedList = [1, "Erlang", {tuple, 1}].

Accessing Elements

To access list elements, predefined functions are used. For example, hd/1 returns the first element, and tl/1 returns the list without the first element:

erlang

Copia

Modifica

FirstElement = hd(ListOfNumbers). % 1

RestOfList = tl(ListOfNumbers). % [2, 3, 4, 5]

List Operations

Erlang provides several functions for manipulating lists. Some examples include:

List Concatenation: An element can be added to the beginning of a list using the | operator, and two lists can be concatenated using the ++ operator.

erlang

Copia

Modifica

ListWithNewElement = [0 | ListOfNumbers].
% [0, 1, 2, 3, 4, 5]

ConcatenatedList = ListOfNumbers ++ [6, 7, 8]. % [1, 2, 3, 4, 5, 6, 7, 8]

Filtering: The lists:filter/2 function allows filtering list elements based on a specified condition.

erlang

Copia

Modifica

FilteredList = lists:filter(fun(X) -> X rem 2 == 0 end, ListOfNumbers).

% Result: [2, 4]

Mapping: The lists:map/2 function applies a function to every element in a list.

erlang

Copia

Modifica

SquaredList = lists:map(fun(X) -> X * X end, ListOfNumbers).

% Result: [1, 4, 9, 16, 25]

5.2 Tuples and Their Usage

Tuples in Erlang are fixed-size data structures that can contain a defined number of elements of any type. Tuples are represented using curly braces {}.

Creating Tuples

Here are some examples of tuples:

erlang

Copia

Modifica

TupleOfNumbers = {1, 2, 3}.

MixedTuple = {a, {b, c}, 3.14}.

Accessing Elements

To access elements in a tuple, the element/2 operator is used, where the first argument is the index (starting at 1) and the second is the tuple:

erlang

Copia

45

Modifica

FirstElement = element(1, TupleOfNumbers).
% 1

SecondElement = element(2,
TupleOfNumbers). % 2

Using Tuples

Tuples are useful for grouping a fixed number of values. For example, tuples can represent coordinates in a 2D system:

erlang

Copia

Modifica

Coordinates = {10, 20}.

5.3 Maps and Key-Value Access

Maps are a data structure introduced in Erlang 17.0 and are similar to objects in other programming languages. Maps allow storing key-value pairs.

Creating Maps

Here are some examples of maps:

erlang

Copia

Modifica

Map = #{ "name" => "Erlang", "year" => 1986 }.

Accessing Elements

To access values in a map, the maps:get/2 operator is used (where the first argument is the key and the second is the map):

erlang

Copia

Modifica

Name = maps:get("name", Map). % "Erlang"

Year = maps:get("year", Map). % 1986

Updating and Deleting

Maps also allow updating values for a specific key with maps:put/3 and removing key-value pairs with maps:remove/2.

erlang

Copia

Modifica

UpdatedMap = maps:put("year", 1987, Map). % Update the year

MapWithoutYear = maps:remove("year", UpdatedMap). % Remove the "year" key

5.4 Properties of Data Structures

Each data structure in Erlang has specific characteristics. Here are some important properties of the data structures we have examined:

Lists: Lists are dynamic and can contain a variable number of elements. However, accessing elements in a list has $O(n)$ complexity because the list must be traversed to find the desired element.

Tuples: Tuples have a fixed size, which means they cannot be resized. Accessing an element in a tuple is $O(1)$, making them very fast.

Maps: Maps are flexible data structures that allow quick access to values using keys. Accessing, updating, and removing elements in a map typically have $O(1)$ complexity.

5.5 Creating and Using Modules

In Erlang, modules are fundamental units for organizing code. A module is a file containing function definitions. Modules allow for better code organization and visibility management for functions.

Creating a Module

A module in Erlang is defined using -module(NameOfModule). at the beginning of the file, followed by a declaration of public functions.

Here's an example of a simple module named math_utils.erl:

erlang

Copia

Modifica

```
-module(math_utils).

-export([sum/2, product/2]).

sum(A, B) ->
A + B.

product(A, B) ->
A * B.
```

In this example, we define a module called math_utils with two public functions: sum/2 and product/2. The numbers after the function name indicate the number of arguments the function accepts.

Compiling a Module

To use a module, it must be compiled. You can do this in the Erlang shell:

shell

Copia

Modifica

```
1> c(math_utils).
{ok,math_utils}
```

Using a Module

Once compiled, you can use the functions defined in the module. Here's how to use math_utils:

erlang

Copia

Modifica

```
SumResult = math_utils:sum(5, 3). % Result: 8

ProductResult = math_utils:product(4, 2). % Result: 8
```

Modules and Namespace Management

Modules in Erlang provide isolation between

functions. Functions with the same name in different modules can coexist without conflicts, as they are accessed through the module name.

Data structures and modules in Erlang provide a powerful set of tools for managing data and organizing code. Lists, tuples, and maps allow handling information of various forms and sizes, while modules offer a structured way to define and use functions. These elements are fundamental for developing robust and scalable applications in Erlang.

Chapter 6: Applications of Erlang

Erlang is a programming language designed for building robust and scalable systems, particularly suitable for applications requiring high concurrency, fault tolerance, and distribution. Initially developed for the telecommunications industry, Erlang has found applications across a wide range of domains. In this section, we will explore some of Erlang's primary applications, including server and client development, distributed applications, and interactions with databases like Mnesia.

6.1 Developing Servers

Erlang is particularly well-suited for server development due to its concurrent architecture. Applications written in Erlang can handle thousands of simultaneous connections without significant performance degradation. This capability is enabled by lightweight processes and actor-based concurrency management.

Example: Simple TCP Server

A basic TCP server in Erlang can be implemented using the `gen_tcp` module. This server listens for incoming connections and responds with a greeting message.

```erlang
-module(simple_tcp_server).
-export([start/1, accept/1]).

start(Port) ->
{ok, ListenSocket} = gen_tcp:listen(Port, [binary, {active, false}]),
accept(ListenSocket).

accept(ListenSocket) ->
{ok, Socket} = gen_tcp:accept(ListenSocket),
spawn(fun() -> handle_client(Socket) end),
accept(ListenSocket).

handle_client(Socket) ->
gen_tcp:send(Socket, <<"Welcome to the TCP server!">>),
gen_tcp:close(Socket).
```

In this example, the server listens on a specified port and accepts incoming connections, handling each client in a separate process. The `handle_client/1` function sends a welcome message to the client and closes the connection.

Benefits of Servers in Erlang

1. **Concurrency**: Erlang allows managing thousands of lightweight processes running simultaneously.

2. **Fault Tolerance**: If a process encounters an error, others continue to operate without interruption.

3. **Simplicity**: The language's architecture simplifies handling network connections and data.

6.2 Developing Clients

While Erlang is often considered a server-side language, it is also well-suited for developing clients that interface with remote servers. An Erlang client can connect to servers, send requests, and receive responses.

Example: Simple TCP Client

Here's how a basic TCP client might look when connecting to the previously created server:

```erlang
-module(simple_tcp_client).
-export([start/2]).

start(Host, Port) ->
    {ok, Socket} = gen_tcp:connect(Host, Port, []),
    gen_tcp:recv(Socket, 0),
    gen_tcp:close(Socket).
```

In this example, the client connects to a specified host and port, receives a message sent by the server, and then closes the connection.

Benefits of Clients in Erlang

1. **Ease of Connection**: Erlang provides simple interfaces for establishing network connections.

2. **Error Handling**: Erlang's error model makes handling network issues, like

connection timeouts, straightforward.

3. **Integration with Existing Systems**:
With support for common protocols like TCP
and HTTP, Erlang can easily integrate with
other systems.

6.3 Distributed Applications

Erlang's ability to handle distributed processes
and inter-machine communication is one of its
strongest features. Applications written in
Erlang can easily scale horizontally across
multiple nodes, distributing the workload
efficiently.

Example: Distributed Application with
`global`

One of Erlang's features is the ability to use
the `global` module to manage process
registration across nodes. This facilitates
creating applications that can communicate
and share states.

```erlang
-module(distributed_example).

-export([start/0, worker/0]).
```

```
start() ->

global:register_name(my_worker, spawn(fun worker/0)).

worker() ->

receive

{msg, Message} ->

io:format("Received message: ~s~n", [Message]),

worker()

end.
```
```

In this example, the `worker` process is globally registered, allowing other nodes to send messages to it.

#### Benefits of Distributed Applications in Erlang

1. **Transparency**: Processes can communicate without concern for whether they are on the same machine.

2. **Scalability**: Adding new nodes to the network is straightforward, enabling both vertical and horizontal scaling.
```

3. **Fault Tolerance**: If a node fails, other nodes can continue to function.

6.4 Interactions with Databases (e.g., Mnesia)

Erlang is often used with the Mnesia database, a distributed and management-oriented database designed specifically for systems written in Erlang. Mnesia is highly beneficial for applications requiring fast and distributed data management.

Example: Using Mnesia

Here is a simple example of interacting with Mnesia. In this example, we create a table, insert data, and then retrieve it.

```erlang
-module(mnesia_example).

-export([start/0, create_table/0, insert_data/0, fetch_data/0]).

start() ->

mnesia:start(),

create_table(),
```

```erlang
insert_data(),

fetch_data().

create_table() ->

mnesia:create_schema([node()]),

mnesia:start(),

mnesia:create_table(users, [{attributes,
record_info(fields, user)}]).

-record(user, {id, name}).

insert_data() ->

mnesia:transaction(fun() ->

mnesia:write(#user{id=1, name="Mario"}),

mnesia:write(#user{id=2, name="Luigi"})

end).

fetch_data() ->

Result = mnesia:transaction(fun() ->

mnesia:match_object(#user{id = '_', name =
'_'})

end),

case Result of

{atomic, Data} -> io:format("Data: ~p~n",
[Data]);
```

```erlang
        _ -> io:format("Error retrieving data~n")
    end.
```

In this example, we create a Mnesia schema and a `users` table, insert some records, and then fetch the data for display.

Benefits of Mnesia

1. **In-memory and Persistent**: Mnesia can operate as both an in-memory and persistent database, offering flexibility.

2. **Distributed**: Mnesia supports distribution, allowing multiple nodes to access the data.

3. **Ease of Use**: Mnesia is integrated into Erlang, making it simple and intuitive for developers familiar with the language.

Erlang has proven to be a powerful and versatile language for developing servers, clients, distributed applications, and database interactions. Its unique design, centered on concurrency and fault tolerance, makes it ideal for modern software systems that demand robustness, scalability, and manageability. With a vibrant ecosystem and active community, Erlang continues to be an excellent choice for developers tackling the challenges of the future in programming.

Chapter 7 Testing and Debugging in Erlang

Testing and debugging are fundamental parts of the software development lifecycle, especially in a language like Erlang, which is designed for building distributed and self-healing systems. The robustness and resilience of applications written in Erlang largely depend on the quality of testing and the ability to diagnose and resolve issues when they arise. This chapter explores the main aspects of testing and debugging in Erlang, focusing on unit tests, debugging tools, performance profiling, and application monitoring.

7.1 Unit Testing in Erlang

Unit testing is an essential practice to ensure that individual pieces of code work as expected. In Erlang, the most common testing framework is `EUnit`, which is built into the language and provides a simple way to write and organize tests.

Writing Tests with EUnit

Here is an example of how to write a unit test

using `EUnit`. Suppose we have a simple module called `math_ops` containing a function to add two numbers:

```erlang
-module(math_ops).

-export([add/2]).

add(A, B) ->

A + B.
```

To test this function, we can create a test module as follows:

```erlang
-module(math_ops_tests).

-include_lib("eunit/include/eunit.hrl").

add_test_() ->

?assertEqual(3, math_ops:add(1, 2)),

?assertEqual(0, math_ops:add(1, -1)),

?assertEqual(5, math_ops:add(2, 3)).
```

Running the Tests

To run the tests, simply compile and load the modules in an Erlang shell, then call the test module:

```erlang
1> c(math_ops).
{ok,math_ops}.
2> c(math_ops_tests).
{ok,math_ops_tests}.
3> math_ops_tests:test().
```

This will return the test results, indicating which tests passed and which failed.

Testing Concurrent Functions

Erlang is designed for concurrent programming, so it is important to test code that interacts with multiple processes. For example, if we have a function that spawns a process to compute a value, we can write a test to ensure the process returns the expected result:

```erlang
-module(concurrent_ops).
-export([async_add/2]).
async_add(A, B) ->
```

```erlang
Pid = spawn(fun() -> A + B end),
receive
Result -> Result
end.
```

The test for this function might look like this:

```erlang
async_add_test_() ->
?assertEqual(3, concurrent_ops:async_add(1, 2)).
```

Mocking in Unit Tests

Sometimes, you may need to mock functions or entire modules to test code in isolation. In Erlang, you can use external libraries such as `Mox` to handle mocking. Mocking allows you to simulate the behavior of other functions without executing them, enabling testing without external dependencies.

7.2 Debugging Tools

Debugging is a crucial aspect of software development. Erlang offers several tools to facilitate the discovery and resolution of issues in code.

Erlang Debugger

Erlang's built-in debugger is a visual tool that allows you to inspect running code. You can start it from the Erlang shell with the command `debugger:start()`. This tool enables you to load the module to debug, set breakpoints, step through code, and monitor variables.

Example usage of the debugger:

1. Start the debugger:

```erlang
1> debugger:start().
```

2. Load the module:

```erlang
2> debugger:load_module(math_ops).
```

3. Set a breakpoint:

```erlang
3> debugger:break(math_ops, add, 1).
```

```

```

4. Execute a function that calls `math_ops:add/2`. When it reaches the breakpoint, you can examine the process state and variables.

`sys:trace` and Process Monitoring

Another powerful debugging tool is `sys:trace/3`, which allows you to monitor function calls, messaging, and more. For instance, to see which functions are being called within a process, you can use:

```erlang
sys:trace(Pid, true).
```

This activates tracing for the process with ID `Pid`. Use `false` to deactivate tracing. `trace` is useful for diagnosing complex logic issues or monitoring process interactions.

Logging and Tracing

In addition to the debugger, logging is a valuable tool for debugging. You can use Erlang's logging library to record events and application states.

Example:
```erlang
-include_lib("logger/include/logger.hrl").

log_example() ->

logger:notice("Starting calculation..."),

Result = math_ops:add(1, 2),

logger:info("Calculation result: ~p", [Result]),

Result.
```

Breakpoints and Hot Code Reloading

Erlang developers can leverage hot code reloading to apply changes to code without stopping the application. During debugging, you can use breakpoints to examine the code execution in real-time. This provides significant productivity benefits.

7.3 Performance Profiling

Profiling is critical for identifying bottlenecks in application performance. Erlang offers various tools for profiling.

`eprof`

`eprof` is a built-in library for time profiling in

Erlang. It helps identify which function consumes the most execution time.

Example:

```erlang
eprof:apply(math_ops, add, [1, 2]).
```

After running the function, view the profiling results:

```erlang
eprof:stop().

eprof:analyse().
```

This analysis provides a detailed report on where time was spent during execution.

`fprof`

`fprof` is a more advanced library that provides detailed information about function calls. You can use it to measure the execution time of each function in a particular call, creating a detailed performance profile.

External Monitoring Tools

In addition to built-in tools, external

monitoring tools such as `Observer` provide graphical views of application performance. Start it with:

```erlang
observer:start().
```

`Observer` offers insights into active processes, memory usage, load distribution, and other key metrics.

7.4 Application Monitoring

Application monitoring is essential to ensure systems are running as expected and to gather resource usage statistics.

Supervisors and Process Monitoring

In a distributed architecture, supervisors can be used to monitor processes and restart them in case of failure. Each time a child process crashes, the supervisor can automatically restart it or take other actions, such as logging the error or sending a notification.

Defining a supervision strategy is key to ensuring the system remains operational even in the face of unexpected failures.

```erlang
supervise_children() ->

{ok, Pid} = supervisor:start_link({local,
my_supervisor},

{simple_one_for_one, 5}),

supervisor:start_child(Pid, {my_worker, []}).
```

Metrics and Health Checks

Using libraries like `telemetry`, you can collect real-time metrics from your Erlang application. These metrics can then be sent to an external monitoring service for deeper analysis.

Application Logs

Finally, implementing a robust logging system is critical for monitoring the state of your application. A well-designed logging system allows you to track operations and quickly identify issues. Consider using logging libraries like Lager to manage logs efficiently.

In the world of Erlang, where robustness, resilience, and concurrency management are core business, testing and debugging are not just auxiliary practices but crucial foundations of the application development lifecycle. Unit testing techniques with `EUnit`, debugging tools like `debugger` and `eprof`, and active monitoring and logging practices are essential to ensure that applications not only work as expected but also respond efficiently in complex scenarios.

By committing to properly testing and monitoring your Erlang application, you can minimize issues, improve performance, and deliver a better user experience. Implementing robust testing, monitoring tools, and debugging techniques will set you on the path to developing and maintaining scalable and robust applications.

Chapter 8: Tools and Development Environment

Erlang is a programming language designed for building distributed, fault-tolerant, and scalable systems. To facilitate the development and management of Erlang projects, having the right tools and a suitable development environment is essential. In this chapter, we will explore various aspects of tools and the environment for programming in Erlang, including how to install Erlang and OTP, use the Erlang Shell interpreter, build and manage projects, and choose the best editors or IDEs.

8.1 Installing Erlang and OTP

8.1.1 What is OTP?

Erlang is a programming language developed by Ericsson in the 1980s, designed for developing telecommunication systems. OTP, which stands for Open Telecom Platform, is a collection of libraries and design principles that extend the Erlang language. OTP provides tools and structures for handling concurrency, fault tolerance, and distribution.

8.1.2 Installation on Various Operating Systems

Installing on Linux

Most Linux distributions have precompiled packages for Erlang. Here's how to install it on one of the most popular distributions, Ubuntu:

1. **Update the package list:**

```bash
sudo apt-get update
```

2. **Install Erlang:**

```bash
sudo apt-get install erlang
```

3. **Verify the installation:**

```bash
erl
```

You should see information about the Erlang

version.

Installing on macOS

On macOS, you can use Homebrew to manage the installation:

1. **Install Homebrew (if not already installed):**

```bash
/bin/bash -c "$(curl -fsSL https://raw.githubusercontent.com/Homebrew/install/HEAD/install.sh)"
```

2. **Install Erlang:**

```bash
brew install erlang
```

3. **Verify the installation:**

```bash
erl
```

Installing on Windows

To install Erlang on Windows, download the

installer from the official website:

1. **Visit the Erlang website:**

Go to [Erlang's official website]
(https://www.erlang.org/downloads).

2. **Download the appropriate installer for Windows.**

3. **Run the installer and follow the instructions.**

4. **Verify the installation:**

Open the Windows terminal and type:

```bash
erl
```

8.2 Using the Erlang Shell

Once Erlang is installed, you can start the Erlang Shell by typing `erl` at the command line. The Erlang Shell is an interactive interpreter that allows you to easily experiment with Erlang.

8.2.1 Basic Commands

Executing a Simple Expression

You can execute simple mathematical

expressions directly in the shell:

```erlang
1 + 2.
```

Output:

```
3
```

Defining Functions

You can also define functions in the shell:

```erlang
1> my_function(X) -> X * X.
```

And call the function:

```erlang
2> my_function(5).
```

Output:

```
25
```

```
```

8.2.2 Modules and Compilation

You can also create modules in a separate file and compile them directly in the shell. Save the following code in a file named `math_ops.erl`:

```erlang
-module(math_ops).

-export([square/1]).

square(X) -> X * X.
```

In the shell, load the module:

```erlang
1> c(math_ops).
```

Output:

```
{ok,math_ops}
```

And call the function:

```erlang
```

```
2> math_ops:square(4).
```

Output:
```

16
```

8.3 Building and Managing Projects

Project management in Erlang can be achieved using tools like Relx and Rebar3.

8.3.1 Relx and Rebar3

Rebar3

Rebar3 is a build tool for Erlang that provides all the functionalities needed for project management. Rebar3 simplifies the process of configuration, compilation, and dependency management.

Installing Rebar3

You can install Rebar3 using the following commands:

```bash
# If Erlang is installed:
```

```
wget https://s3.amazonaws.com/rebar3/rebar3
chmod +x rebar3
sudo mv rebar3 /usr/local/bin/
```

Creating a New Project

To create a new project, use the command:

```bash
rebar3 new app my_app
```

This will create a new folder `my_app` with a predefined project structure.

Compiling the Project

Navigate to your project folder and compile:

```bash
cd my_app
rebar3 compile
```

Adding Dependencies

You can add dependencies in the `rebar.config` file. For example:

```erlang
{deps, [
{cowboy, "2.7.0"}
]}.
```

After adding dependencies, run:

```bash
rebar3 get-deps
```

Relx

Relx is another tool for building and releasing Erlang projects, particularly useful for creating deployable packages.

Creating a Release

To use Relx, you need a `relx.config` file. Assuming you have an app called `my_app`, the `relx.config` file might look like this:

```erlang
{release, {my_app, "0.1.0"},
[
my_app,
```

my_dep

]}.

```

To build the release, use the Relx commands:

```bash

relx build

```

This will generate a directory structure for the deployable app.

8.4 Recommended IDEs and Editors

Choosing a good editor or IDE is crucial for effective development in Erlang. Below are some popular options.

8.4.1 Visual Studio Code

Visual Studio Code (VS Code) is a very popular source code editor. With the Erlang extension, it supports syntax highlighting, autocomplete, and other utilities.

Installing the Erlang Extension

1. Open VS Code.

2. Go to "Extensions" (Ctrl+Shift+X).
```

3. Search for "Erlang" and install the extension.

8.4.2 IntelliJ IDEA

IntelliJ IDEA is a powerful IDE. Combining advanced refactoring features and good support for various languages, it also supports Erlang through plugins.

Installing the Erlang Plugin

1. Open IntelliJ IDEA.

2. Go to "File" > "Settings" > "Plugins".

3. Search for "Erlang" and install the plugin.

8.4.3 Emacs

Emacs is a highly customizable text editor. With the right set of packages, it can become a powerful development environment for Erlang.

Setting Up Erlang in Emacs

You can use `erlang.el` to enable Erlang support in Emacs. Install it using your preferred package manager.

8.4.4 Vim

Vim is another popular editor among

developers. With proper configurations and plugins, it can fully support Erlang.

Erlang Plugin for Vim

You can use the `vim-erlang-runtime` plugin. Add the following line to your `.vimrc`:

```vim
Plugin 'eraserhd/parinfer-racket-vim'
```

In this chapter, we covered various aspects of tools and the development environment for Erlang. Installing Erlang and OTP, using the Erlang Shell, building and managing projects with tools like Relx and Rebar3, and choosing suitable IDEs and editors are all critical for working effectively with Erlang. With a solid understanding of these tools, developers can create scalable and resilient applications using Erlang's powerful ecosystem.

Chapter 9: Advanced Concepts in Erlang

In this chapter, we will delve into some of the more advanced features of Erlang. These include advanced functional programming, design patterns, the implementation of Finite State Machines (FSMs), interoperability with other languages through NIF and Port, and finally, performance optimization. Each section will include explanatory details and practical examples to aid comprehension.

9.1 Advanced Functional Programming

Functional programming is at the core of Erlang and offers many advanced concepts that can be leveraged to write more robust and efficient code. These include higher-order functions, currying, and lazy evaluation.

Higher-Order Functions

Higher-order functions are functions that can take other functions as arguments or return functions as results. This enables highly reusable code.

Example:

```erlang
% Define a function that applies a given function to each element of a list
apply_function(List, Func) ->
lists:map(Func, List).

% Define a function that doubles a number
double(X) ->
X * 2.

% Use apply_function
Result = apply_function([1, 2, 3, 4], fun double/1).

% Result will be [2, 4, 6, 8]
```

Currying

Currying is a technique that transforms a function with multiple arguments into a series of unary functions, each taking a single argument. Although Erlang doesn't directly support currying, a similar effect can be achieved by returning functions.

Example:

```erlang
% Function that returns a function adding a
number to another

add(X) ->

fun(Y) -> X + Y end.

% Using the function

add_five = add(5).

Result = add_five(10).

% Result will be 15
```

Lazy Evaluation

While Erlang primarily uses eager execution,
lazy evaluation can be simulated using
anonymous functions and lists.

Example:

```erlang
% Function that generates an infinite list of
numbers

infinite_numbers(N) ->

[N | infinite_numbers(N + 1)].

% Take only the first N numbers
```

```erlang
take(N, List) ->
lists:take(N, List).
% Usage
List = infinite_numbers(1),
TopFive = take(5, List).
% TopFive will be [1, 2, 3, 4, 5]
```

9.2 Design Patterns in Erlang

Design patterns help solve common problems in software development. In Erlang, many of these patterns stem from concurrent and distributed programming paradigms.

Parent-Child Pattern

In Erlang, the process model is fundamental. Processes can communicate through messages, and the parent-child pattern dictates how one process can supervise others. This is often used to ensure application resilience.

Example:

```erlang
% A parent that starts a child process and
```

monitors its termination

```erlang
start_child() ->
Pid = spawn(fun child_process/0),
monitor(process, Pid),
{ok, Pid}.
child_process() ->
receive
stop -> ok
end.
```

State Machine Pattern

Finite State Machines (FSMs) are excellent for managing orderly state transitions. These can be implemented in Erlang using recursion and messages.

Example:

```erlang
% Simple FSM
fsm(State) ->
receive
next ->
```

```
NewState = case State of

state1 -> state2;

state2 -> state1

end,

fsm(NewState);

stop ->

ok

end.
```
\`\`\`

9.3 Finite State Machines in Erlang

FSMs are a great way to model complex behaviors in Erlang programs. They can be implemented using processes and messages for clarity and precision.

Example: Classic FSM

Consider a traffic light with three states: red, yellow, and green. Each state lasts for a specific duration before transitioning to the next.

Example:

```erlang
% Traffic light states and durations
traffic_light(red) ->
timer:sleep(2000), % Red for 2 seconds
traffic_light(green);
traffic_light(green) ->
timer:sleep(3000), % Green for 3 seconds
traffic_light(yellow);
traffic_light(yellow) ->
timer:sleep(1000), % Yellow for 1 second
traffic_light(red).
% Start the traffic light
start_traffic_light() ->
spawn(fun() -> traffic_light(red) end).
```

9.4 Interoperability with Other Languages (NIF, Port)

Erlang provides several ways to interact with other programming languages using NIF (Native Implemented Functions) and Port.

These methods enable developers to utilize libraries written in C, C++, or other languages.

NIF (Native Implemented Functions)

NIFs are C functions that can be directly called from Erlang. They allow performance-intensive operations to be optimized.

Example:

```c
#include "erl_nif.h"

// NIF function to add two numbers

static ERL_NIF_TERM add(ErlNifEnv* env, int argc, const ERL_NIF_TERM argv[]) {

int a, b;

if (!enif_get_int(env, argv[0], &a) || ! enif_get_int(env, argv[1], &b)) {

return enif_make_badarg(env);

}

return enif_make_int(env, a + b);

}

static ErlNifFunc nif_funcs[] = {
```

```
  {"add", 2, add}
};
ERL_NIF_INIT(Elixir.MyModule, nif_funcs,
NULL, NULL, NULL, NULL)
```

Port

Ports allow external programs (written in C, Python, etc.) to communicate with Erlang code. This is useful when keeping logic in a separate language while ensuring efficient interaction.

Example:

```erlang
% Use a Port to send and receive messages
start_port() ->

Port = open_port({spawn,
"external_program"}, [stream, use_stdio,
exit_status]),

Port ! {self(), {command, "hello"}},

receive

{Port, {data, Result}} -> io:format("Received:
~s\n", [Result])
```

end.
```
```

9.5 Performance Optimization

Performance optimization in Erlang can target various aspects, from concurrency management to memory optimization.

Concurrency

Erlang is designed for massive concurrency. Using lightweight processes and message passing is key. Avoid global variables and shared memory to maintain performance.

Profiling

Profiling the application is a good starting point to identify improvement areas. Erlang includes tools for measuring application performance.

Example:

```erlang
% Start profiling
app:start().

prof:run(fun my_function/0).
```

Minimizing Garbage Collection

Efficient memory management and minimizing garbage collection operations can significantly improve performance.

- Partition data into minimal structures.

- Avoid passing large, unnecessary data structures.

Through this chapter, we explored several advanced concepts in Erlang, from functional programming techniques, design patterns, FSM implementation, interoperability with other languages, to performance optimization techniques. These tools and techniques not only improve code efficiency but also enhance the robustness and resilience of applications developed in Erlang.

Chapter 10: Building Applications in Erlang

Erlang is a programming language specifically designed for building distributed and fault-tolerant systems. Its robustness, concurrency handling, and ease of development make it ideal for creating scalable and resilient applications. In this chapter, we will explore step-by-step how to build an application using Erlang, covering planning, setting up the environment, writing code, testing practices, and deployment.

Step 1: Plan the Application

Before writing any code, it is crucial to have a clear vision of the application you want to develop. During this phase, consider the following points:

1. **Application Goals**: What is the purpose of the application? Examples include a chat app, a web server, or an event management system.

2. **Functional and Non-Functional

Requirements**: What are the main features? Is zero downtime essential? What are the performance requirements?

3. **Overall Architecture**: How will the system be structured? What modules are needed? How will they communicate?

For instance, let's imagine building a real-time chat application. The requirements might include sending messages, creating rooms, managing connected users, and ensuring message reliability.

Step 2: Set Up the Development Environment

To develop in Erlang, you need the Erlang runtime and some supporting tools. Follow these steps:

1. **Install Erlang**: Download Erlang from the [official site] (https://www.erlang.org/downloads) and follow the installation instructions for your operating system.

2. **Choose a Text Editor**: Use an IDE like Visual Studio Code with Erlang support or a

text editor like Vim or Emacs.

3. **Configure the Environment**: In your terminal, verify the Erlang installation by running `erl`, which should start the Erlang shell.

Step 3: Build the Application

3.1: Create the Basic Structure

Erlang applications are organized into modules. Here's how you can set up a basic structure for our chat application:

1. **Create a New Application Folder**:

```bash
mkdir chat_app
cd chat_app
```

2. **Create a Module for Chat Room Management**: Create a file named `chat_room.erl`.

```erlang
-module(chat_room).
-export([start/0, join/1, send_message/2,
```

```erlang
get_messages/0]).

start() ->
    {ok, spawn(fun loop/0)}.

loop() ->
    receive
        {join, User} ->
            %% Logic for handling user joining
            io:format("~s joined the chat room.~n", [User]),
            loop();
        {message, User, Msg} ->
            %% Logic for handling message sending
            io:format("~s says: ~s~n", [User, Msg]),
            loop()
    end.
```

In this simple module, we create a chat room, allow users to join, and send messages.

3.2: Create the Main Module

Now, create a main module that coordinates the application. Name the file `chat_server.erl`.

```erlang
-module(chat_server).

-export([start/0, stop/0, join/1, send_message/2]).

start() ->

chat_room:start().

stop() ->

%% Logic to stop the server

ok.

join(User) ->

%% Logic to join the chat

chat_room:join(User).

send_message(User, Msg) ->

chat_room:send_message(User, Msg).
```

This module provides the interfaces that other modules or users can use to interact with the chat system.

3.3: Create a Simple Client

To test our server, let's create a simple client that can input commands. Name the file `chat_client.erl`.

```erlang
-module(chat_client).
-export([start/0]).
start() ->
chat_server:start(),
loop().
loop() ->
io:format("Enter your username: "),
User = io:get_line(""),
UserStr = string:trim(User),
io:format("You have joined as ~s.~n", [UserStr]),
io:format("Type your messages below.~n"),
send_messages(UserStr).
send_messages(User) ->
```

Message = io:get_line(""),

chat_server:send_message(User,
string:trim(Message)),

send_messages(User).
```

This client connects to the server and allows
users to send messages.

---

#### Step 4: Test the Application

With the modules ready, it's time to test the
system. Since Erlang strongly supports
concurrency, you can run multiple client
instances in parallel.

1. Start the server in one Erlang shell:

```bash

erl -s chat_server
```

2. Open additional Erlang shells to start
multiple client instances, for example:

```bash

erl -s chat_client

```
```

3. In each client shell, enter a username and start sending messages. Messages should appear across all shells.

Step 5: Maintain and Add Features

Once the basic application is running, consider adding more features and improvements. Suggestions include:

- **Message Persistence**: Save messages to a database or files.

- **Error Handling**: Implement error-handling strategies to ensure the application can recover from unexpected situations.

- **Security**: Add security by encrypting messages or implementing user authentication.

Step 6: Deploy the Application

Finally, deploy your Erlang application:

1. **Compile**: Use `erlc` to compile your modules.

```bash
erlc chat_room.erl chat_server.erl
chat_client.erl
```

2. **Run in Production**: Use a server or cloud service, install Erlang, and load your modules.

3. **Monitoring and Logging**: Implement logging to track application activity and facilitate maintenance.

In this chapter, we covered the essential steps to develop and deploy a simple chat application in Erlang. We explored planning, environment setup, code writing, testing, and deployment.

Erlang offers numerous opportunities for improving and expanding applications. Once your application is up and running, think about how it can evolve to meet future needs. With a solid foundation and good development practices, you can build reliable and scalable systems using Erlang.

Glossary

This glossary provides a comprehensive list of terms, concepts, and constructs related to the Erlang programming language. Erlang is a functional, concurrent programming language designed for building distributed and fault-tolerant systems. Its ecosystem includes unique features that require a deep understanding of specific terminology. Below, you'll find explanations and examples to help clarify these terms.

A

Actor Model: A computational model used by Erlang where independent entities, called processes, communicate by sending and receiving messages. This model avoids shared memory and ensures fault tolerance. Each actor (or process) has its own state and mailbox.

Application: A collection of modules, processes, and resources packaged together to perform a specific task in Erlang. Applications are commonly defined in a file ending with `.app`.

Arity: The number of arguments a function takes. For example, `sum/2` indicates a function named `sum` with an arity of 2 (two arguments).

Atom: A constant whose name is its value. Atoms are often used as identifiers or keys. Example: `my_atom` or `:ok`.

B

Behaviour: A predefined module interface in Erlang that defines a set of callback functions that a module must implement. Common behaviours include `gen_server`, `gen_statem`, and `supervisor`.

Binary: A sequence of bytes used for efficient storage and manipulation of raw data. Binary literals are written as `<<1, 2, 3>>`.

Bitstring: A contiguous sequence of bits that is a generalization of binaries. Bitstrings are defined with a size in bits.

C

Callback Module: A module that implements the required callback functions for a behaviour. For instance, a module implementing `gen_server` must define functions like `init/1`, `handle_call/3`, and `terminate/2`.

Concurrency: The ability to execute multiple processes simultaneously. In Erlang, concurrency is achieved using lightweight processes.

Core: Refers to the central part of the Erlang runtime system, including the scheduler and the virtual machine (BEAM).

Critical Section: A part of a program that must not be accessed by more than one process at a time. Erlang avoids critical sections through message-passing instead of shared memory.

Curried Function: A function derived from another function by fixing one or more arguments. Erlang doesn't natively support currying but achieves similar results through closures.

D

Daemon: A background process that runs continuously to perform specific tasks, often implemented as a supervisor or `gen_server` in Erlang.

Dets: Short for "Disk Erlang Term Storage," a storage system for large datasets that fit on disk but not entirely in memory. Commonly used in applications that require persistence.

Distributed Erlang: The capability of Erlang nodes to communicate across different machines. Distributed Erlang uses the `net_adm` and `net_kernel` modules for node connections.

Dynamic Typing: Erlang is dynamically typed, meaning types are determined at runtime rather than compile-time. Type mismatches result in runtime errors.

E

ETS (Erlang Term Storage): An in-memory database used for storing large amounts of data. ETS tables can be accessed by multiple processes and are often used for caching and state management.

Erlang Shell: An interactive REPL (Read-Eval-Print Loop) environment for testing and executing Erlang code directly. Start it by typing `erl` in the terminal.

Error Handling: Erlang employs a "let it crash" philosophy where processes are designed to fail and recover gracefully through supervisors.

Export: The process of making specific functions accessible to other modules. Declared with the `-export` attribute. Example: `-export([function_name/arity]).`

Expressions: Units of code that produce a value. Erlang's syntax revolves around expressions rather than statements.

F

Fault Tolerance: The ability of a system to continue functioning even when parts fail. Erlang achieves fault tolerance through supervision trees and process isolation.

Finite State Machine (FSM): A model of

computation implemented in Erlang using the `gen_statem` behaviour. FSMs are used to represent systems with finite states and transitions.

Fun: Short for "function," specifically anonymous functions in Erlang. Declared using the `fun` keyword. Example: `Fun = fun(X) -> X * 2 end.`

G

Garbage Collection: Automatic memory management performed on each Erlang process individually. This minimizes pauses and improves real-time performance.

gen_server: A generic server behaviour module for implementing server processes. It provides a framework for request-response and state management patterns.

Guard: A condition in function clauses or case expressions used to refine pattern matching. Example: `f(X) when X > 0 -> ...`.

H

Hot Code Loading: The ability to update code in a running Erlang system without stopping it. Achieved by loading new versions of modules dynamically.

Heap: The memory area where each Erlang process stores its data. Each process has its own heap to ensure isolation.

High Availability: The ability of a system to remain operational for extended periods, even during hardware or software failures. Erlang's features like process isolation and distributed systems support contribute to high availability.

I

Immutable Data: Data in Erlang is immutable, meaning it cannot be modified once created. New data structures are created when modifications are needed.

Inter-process Communication (IPC): Communication between processes in Erlang is achieved through message passing. This is a core feature of the language.

Interface: Defines how modules interact with each other. For example, callback modules define specific interfaces for behaviours.

J

Join: Refers to the act of connecting processes or nodes. In distributed Erlang, nodes join a cluster to enable communication.

K

Kernel: The core set of libraries and modules in Erlang, including `erlang`, `os`, and `timer`, which provide essential functionalities.

Key-Value Store: A common data storage pattern supported in Erlang via ETS, `maps`, and third-party databases like Mnesia.

L

Lightweight Process: Erlang processes are lightweight, with low memory overhead and fast context switching. Thousands or even millions of processes can run simultaneously.

List Comprehension: A concise way to create lists in Erlang based on existing lists or generators. Example: `[X || X <- List, X > 10].`

Load Balancing: Distributing workloads across multiple nodes or processes. Erlang's distribution and supervision mechanisms facilitate load balancing.

M

Mnesia: A distributed database management system included with Erlang. Mnesia supports transactions and fault-tolerant storage.

Module: The fundamental building block of Erlang programs. Each `.erl` file defines a module. Functions in a module are called as `module_name:function_name/arity`.

Message Passing: The primary method of communication between processes. Messages are sent using `!` and received using `receive` blocks.

Monitored Process: A process that is

being observed by another process. If the monitored process dies, the observing process receives a message.

N

Node: An instance of the Erlang runtime system running on a machine. Distributed systems consist of multiple nodes communicating with each other.

NIF (Native Implemented Function): Functions written in C or another language and loaded into Erlang to optimize performance-critical operations.

Non-blocking: Erlang processes use non-blocking operations to ensure the responsiveness of systems.

O

OTP (Open Telecom Platform): A collection of libraries, tools, and design principles for building Erlang applications. OTP behaviours like `gen_server` and `supervisor` are part of this framework.

Observer: A GUI tool in Erlang for monitoring and debugging live systems. Observer provides insights into process states, memory usage, and more.

P

Pattern Matching: A powerful feature in Erlang for deconstructing data structures. Example: `[Head | Tail] = List` assigns the first element to `Head` and the rest to `Tail`.

Pid (Process Identifier): A unique identifier for an Erlang process. PIDs are used to send messages or monitor processes.

Port: An interface to external programs, allowing Erlang to communicate with other systems or devices.

Process: The basic unit of concurrency in Erlang. Each process runs independently and communicates via message passing.

Q

Queue: A data structure often implemented using lists or external libraries in

Erlang. Used for managing ordered tasks or events.

R

Receive: A construct used to handle incoming messages in a process. Example:

```erlang
receive

{Message, Data} -> io:format("Received: ~p~n", [Data])

end.
```

RPC (Remote Procedure Call): A mechanism for invoking functions on a remote node. Erlang supports RPC through the `rpc` module.

Record: A data structure for grouping related data fields. Defined with the `-record` directive. Example:

```erlang
-record(person, {name, age}).
```

S

Scheduler: A component of the Erlang runtime that distributes processes across CPU cores.

Supervisor: A process responsible for monitoring and restarting child processes in case of failure.

State: The internal data held by a process or module. State is often passed explicitly in functional calls.

T

Tail Recursion: A recursion style where the recursive call is the last operation, allowing efficient memory usage.

Tuple: A fixed-size collection of values. Tuples are written as `{Element1, Element2, ...}`.

U

Uptime: The duration for which an Erlang system has been running without failure. High uptime is a goal of fault-tolerant systems.

V

Variable: A named placeholder for data in Erlang. Variables are immutable once bound to a value.

W

Worker: A process or module that performs specific tasks under the supervision of a supervisor.

Workflow: A sequence of operations represented as processes or message exchanges in Erlang.

X

Xref: A cross-referencing tool in Erlang used to analyze module dependencies and ensure proper coding practices.

Y

Yield: The act of a process giving up

control to allow other processes to execute. Erlang's scheduler manages yields transparently.

Z

Zero Downtime: A system design goal achieved through features like hot code loading and distributed operations in Erlang.

This glossary is a comprehensive resource for anyone learning or working with Erlang, enabling better understanding and effective application of its principles.

Index